Published in 2014 by The Rosen Publishing Group, Inc.
29 East 21st Street, New York, NY 10010

Photo Credits: **KEY** tl=top left; tc=top center; tr=top right; cl=center left; bl=bottom left; bc=bottom center; br=bottom right; bg=background
CBT = Corbis; DT = Dreamstime; IQ = Image Quest; iS = istockphoto.com; SH = Shutterstock; SS = Science and Society Picture Library; TF = Topfoto

6cl iS; **7**tl IQ; br iS; **9**tl IQ; **10**tr CBT; **12–13**tc TF; **16**bl SH; **17**bl, br iS; **18**br DT; **22**bl CBT; **24–25**bg SH; **26**bl SS; **28–29**tc CBT; **30**bg SH; **31**bg SH

All illustrations copyright Weldon Owen Pty Ltd

Weldon Owen Pty Ltd
Managing Director: Kay Scarlett
Creative Director: Sue Burk
Publisher: Helen Bateman
Senior Vice President, International Sales: Stuart Laurence
Vice President Sales North America: Ellen Towell
Administration Manager, International Sales: Kristine Ravn

Library of Congress Cataloging-in-Publication Data

McAllan, Kate.
 Arctic and Antarctic habitats / by Kate McAllan.
    pages cm. — (Discovery education: Habitats)
 Includes index.
 ISBN 978-1-4777-1323-5 (library binding) — ISBN 978-1-4777-1481-2 (paperback) — ISBN 978-1-4777-1482-9 (6-pack)
1. Ecology—Polar regions—Juvenile literature. 2. Ecology—Arctic regions—Juvenile literature. 3. Ecology—Antarctica—Juvenile literature. 4. Polar regions—Environmental conditions—Juvenile literature. 5. Arctic regions—Environmental conditions—Juvenile literature. 6. Antarctica—Environmental conditions—Juvenile literature. I. Title.
 QH541.5.P6M43 2014
 577.0911'3—dc23
                              2012043624

Manufactured in the United States of America

CPSIA Compliance Information: Batch #S13PK3: For Further Information contact Rosen Publishing, New York, New York at 1-800-237-9932

HABITATS

ARCTIC AND ANTARCTIC HABITATS

KATE MCALLAN

PowerKiDS press.

New York

Contents

The Arctic

Temperature ranges
Sea ice reflects about 80 percent of sunlight, which keeps Arctic temperatures low all year round. The coldest is about -94°F (-70°C) and the hottest is 36°F (2°C).

The North Pole, Earth's northernmost point, is located in the Arctic Ocean. The Arctic Circle is an imaginary line above which, due to Earth's tilt, there is at least one summer day when the Sun does not set and at least one winter day when it does not rise.

This region is extremely cold because the Sun's rays strike Earth at a low angle. They have to travel farther through the atmosphere and warm a larger area than elsewhere. Around the North Pole, about 3 million square miles (8 million km^2) of ocean is permanently frozen. Each winter, this mass of ice grows, more than doubling by March.

Communities
Ilulissat, Greenland, lies at the mouth of a fjord, which fills with icebergs that fall from a glacier.

Ice fishing
In winter, Inuit fishermen survive by fishing through holes they make in the ice.

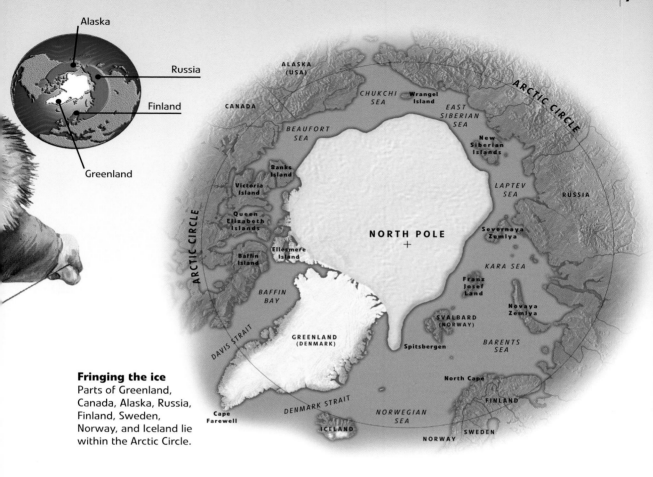

Alaska

Russia

Finland

Greenland

ALASKA
(USA)

CANADA

CHUKCHI
SEA

Wrangel
Island

EAST
SIBERIAN
SEA

ARCTIC CIRCLE

BEAUFORT
SEA

New
Siberian
Islands

Banks
Island

LAPTEV
SEA

RUSSIA

Victoria
Island

Queen
Elizabeth
Islands

ARCTIC CIRCLE

NORTH POLE
+

Severnaya
Zemlya

Baffin
Island

Ellesmere
Island

KARA SEA

BAFFIN
BAY

Franz
Josef
Land

Novaya
Zemlya

DAVIS STRAIT

GREENLAND
(DENMARK)

SVALBARD
(NORWAY)

Spitsbergen

BARENTS
SEA

North Cape

FINLAND

Cape
Farewell

DENMARK STRAIT

ICELAND

NORWEGIAN
SEA

SWEDEN

NORWAY

Fringing the ice
Parts of Greenland,
Canada, Alaska, Russia,
Finland, Sweden,
Norway, and Iceland lie
within the Arctic Circle.

HABITAT CHANGE

Polar bears venture onto sea
ice to hunt for seals, but global
warming means the average
area of sea ice is decreasing.
As the ice diminishes, the bears
cannot reach their food, leading
to a decline in their numbers.

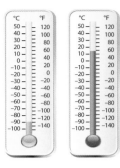

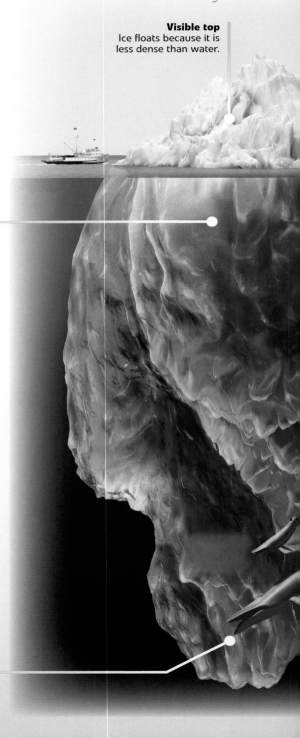

Iceberg
A large piece of floating ice that breaks free from glaciers or ice shelves is called an iceberg.

Visible top
Ice floats because it is less dense than water.

Temperature range
Compared to the Arctic, the temperature in Antarctica is colder in winter but warmer in summer. The coldest is about -128.6°F (-89°C) and the hottest is 59°F (15°C).

Hidden mass
Most of an iceberg floats beneath the sea's surface.

The Antarctic

Earth's southernmost point, the South Pole, is located on the continent of Antarctica. Similar conditions exist within the Antarctic Circle as they do in the Arctic Circle, except it gets colder because the region is dominated by land—there is not as much dark water to absorb heat as in the Arctic.

An ice sheet covers 98 percent of Antarctica. In places, the ice is 2.8 miles (4.5 km) thick. Some of the sea around the continent is frozen all year, but the sea ice grows during winter, reaching its maximum extent in September. There is little life on the continent itself, but the nutrient-rich waters around it support many marine animals.

Fin whales
Fin whales are found mostly in the polar regions.

South America

Africa

Australia

SOUTH SHETLAND
ISLANDS (UK)
Palmer
(USA)
Esperanza
(Argentina)
ELEPHANT
ISLAND (UK)
SOUTH
ORKNEY
ISLANDS
Vernadsky
(Ukraine)
ANTARCTIC
PENINSULA

BELLINGSHAUSEN
SEA

PACIFIC OCEAN

SCOTIA
SEA

AMUNDSEN
SEA

ELLSWORTH
LAND

PALMER
LAND

WEDDELL
SEA

ANTARCTIC CIRCLE

ATLANTIC OCEAN

MARIE
BYRD
LAND

RONNE
ICE SHELF

Halley
(UK)

Belgrano II
(Argentina)

Neumayer
(Germany)

LARSEN ICE
SHELF

Byrd (USA)

ROSS
SEA

ROSS
ICE SHELF

COATS LAND

SOUTH POLE

MCMURDO
SOUND

Scott-Amundsen
(USA)

Troll
(Norway)

Maitri
(India)

Scott
(New Zealand)

McMurdo
(USA)

CAPE
ADARE

QUEEN
MAUD
LAND

Vostok
(Russia)

Mizuho (Japan)

ANTARCTIC CIRCLE

Dumont d'Urville
(France)

WILKES
LAND

LAMBERT
GLACIER

Mawson
(Australia)

Zhongshan
(China)

The lonely continent
Research stations run by
scientists from countries
around the world are the
only settlements in Antarctica.

Casey (Australia)

Mirnyy (Russia)

INDIAN OCEAN

PRYDZ
BAY

Falling snow

GLACIAL ICE FORMATION

Much of the snow that falls in
the Antarctic does not melt.
Fresh snow buries layers of old
snow. The weight of the upper
layers presses down, compacting
the lower layers into solid ice. The
huge pressure on the lower layers
causes the ice to flow downhill
toward the sea, forming glaciers.

Fresh snow

Small ice granules

Firm, or
compacting ice

Solid ice

Plant Life

The polar regions are extremely cold, with months of low light when all water is frozen. Some plants have adapted to these harsh conditions. In Antarctica, about 1 percent of land is ice-free and not too cold and dry to support plant life. There are a few lichens and mosses growing in the summer in sheltered locations. In the Arctic, mosses, lichens, sedges, grasses, and shrubs survive.

Water expands when it freezes, which ruptures most plants' cells, but many polar plants survive. Some have fluids that freeze only at temperatures below -36.4°F (-38°C). Others allow ice to form in the fluid around their cells, keeping the cells themselves from freezing. Plants can grow in summer when light levels are higher, days are long, and the top layer of the ground thaws.

Short summer
Polar plants must grow and reproduce quickly in the brief summer.

ARCTIC TUNDRA

The Arctic tundra is a treeless landscape of low-growing, hardy vegetation. Tundra plants are adapted to take advantage of a growing season only 50 to 60 days long. Some grow in extremely low light conditions. They begin growing early in the summer and flower quickly. Others cannot set seed in the time available. They store energy over several growing seasons and set seed every few years. Some plants, such as the tiny Arctic willow, are extremely long-lived.

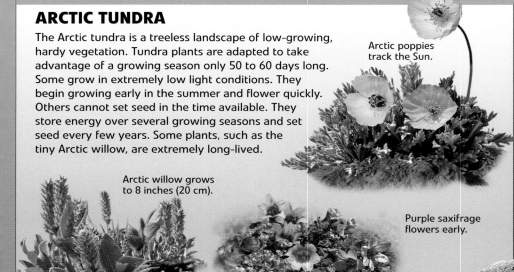

Arctic poppies track the Sun.

Arctic willow grows to 8 inches (20 cm).

Purple saxifrage flowers early.

Safety in numbers
Some Arctic plants grow close together for protection from strong winds.

Trapped fly
Plant hairs bend to hold a trapped insect. The tips of the hairs secrete digestive fluids.

Sticky bait
An insect is attracted by sticky fluid at the base of the hairs on a sundew's leaves.

Leftovers
Nutrients from an insect's soft body parts are absorbed in a few days, leaving only the outer skeleton.

Carnivorous sundews

Like all plants, sundews make proteins from nitrogen. Most plants obtain nitrogen from soil, but sundews get much of theirs from the bodies of insects. This allows them to grow in poor soils.

Herbivores

Tundra vegetation supports many herbivorous mammals, from small lemmings and arctic hares to the massive musk oxen, which weigh in at 900 pounds (410 kg). Some herbivores live in the Arctic all year. A few survive winter by hibernating. Arctic ground squirrels, for instance, hibernate together in a fur-lined burrow. Lemmings occupy tunnels during winter, eating stored seeds and grasses and digging through snow for fresh plant material. The snow insulates them from the cold.

The arctic hare relies on its double-layered coat to survive, crouching with its back to the wind when not feeding. Long outer hair keeps the cold out and a thick undercoat traps heat near its body. These hares stamp their feet and chew through ice to reach plant food. Musk oxen reach their winter food by breaking up ice with their hooves and hard heads.

CARIBOU

Known as reindeer in Europe, caribou spend the summer grazing on the tundra and give birth to their calves there. As winter comes, they migrate south to forest habitats. When they migrate, they often swim over lakes or rivers. Their thick double fur not only keeps them warm on land, it traps air and aids buoyancy in the water.

Caribou scrape snow away to find food.

Reindeer have long been hunted and herded.

Spread toes enable caribou to walk in snow.

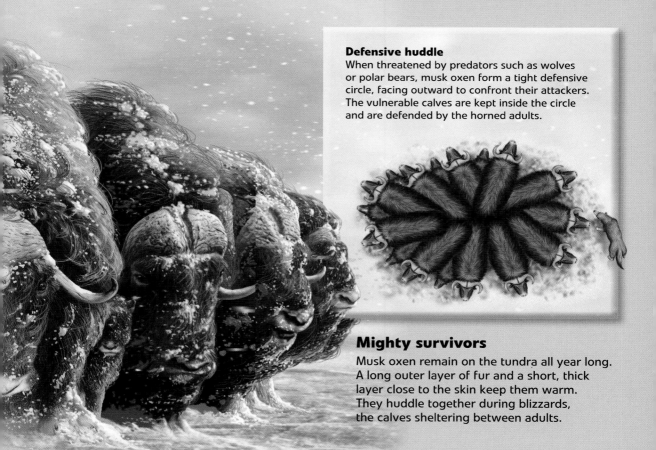

Defensive huddle

When threatened by predators such as wolves or polar bears, musk oxen form a tight defensive circle, facing outward to confront their attackers. The vulnerable calves are kept inside the circle and are defended by the horned adults.

Mighty survivors

Musk oxen remain on the tundra all year long. A long outer layer of fur and a short, thick layer close to the skin keep them warm. They huddle together during blizzards, the calves sheltering between adults.

Small White Hunters

Like many other Arctic animals, the arctic fox is pure white in winter but brown in summer. This allows it to go undetected both by its prey and by predators, such as polar bears and wolves. While there is plenty of small prey available for the arctic fox in summer, in winter it often relies on scavenging from polar bear kills or on surplus food that it buried in the permafrost in summer.

The arctic fox is highly adapted to the cold. Its legs, snout, and ears are short, which means it loses less body heat than other foxes. Its winter fur is the warmest of any animal and is twice as deep as its summer coat. When it sleeps, it wraps its bushy tail over its nose.

Deadly pounce

Arctic foxes prey on small animals, including lemmings. They leap and pounce to break through snow to catch them in winter.

SNOWY OWL

The snowy owl sits on rocks to watch for prey, which include hares, lemmings, and birds. Its ruffled wing feathers allow it to swoop silently. The male is all white. The female is mottled in order to be camouflaged when sitting on her nest on the ground.

Long, thick feathers cover almost all of this owl.

Many Arctic hunters eat lemmings, a type of rodent.

Seasonal changes

In spring, many Arctic animals shed their white fur or feathers and grow a brown or mottled covering. In fall, they molt again. Their brown garb is replaced with a white, thicker covering. This keeps them camouflaged and warm.

Summer stoat

In summer, the stoat is brown with a white underbelly.

Summer kits
The arctic fox has its kits in early summer when food, such as lemmings, young birds, and eggs, is plentiful.

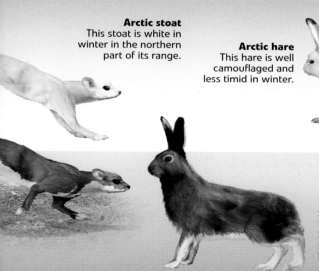

Arctic stoat
This stoat is white in winter in the northern part of its range.

Arctic hare
This hare is well camouflaged and less timid in winter.

Willow ptarmigan
This bird has pure white plumage in winter.

Southern hare
In the far north, this hare is white all year. Farther south, it is brown in summer.

Summer pattern
In summer the ptarmigan has mottled brown feathers. The male has a white underbelly.

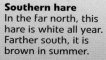

WINTER

SUMMER

Polar Bears

Polar bears are the Arctic's top predators and are the largest carnivores on land. Males can grow up to 11.5 feet (3.5 m) long. They hunt on the sea ice, moving onto land when the ice breaks up in summer. Their prey includes fish, seabirds, seals, beluga whales, and reindeer. One of their main hunting strategies is to wait at a seal's breathing hole in the ice. When a seal appears, they strike it with a massive, clawed forepaw.

Polar bears are well adapted to survive extreme cold. A layer of blubber traps body heat and stores energy. The double-layered fur has water-repellent outer guard hairs and a soft, dense, insulating undercoat. The hairs are also hollow. As sunlight strikes them, heat and light travels to the black skin, where it is absorbed.

The den

In fall, a pregnant female digs a den where, in winter, she gives birth to small, blind cubs. Feeding them fat-rich milk, the mother polar bear herself does not eat.

Tunnel entrance

After winter passes, the mother breaks through the snow covering the entrance and her cubs emerge.

Play and practice

Young wrestling male polar bears are not just playing. They are practicing for the day when they might fight over a female or over food.

INTELLIGENT ORCAS

Orcas, the largest toothed whales, live in all the world's oceans, including those of the polar regions. They often hunt in groups, and their strategies include tipping ice floes to force seals or penguins back into the water where they can be caught.

Orcas can hold themselves vertical to look above the surface of the water for prey.

Breaching humpback

The humpback, a baleen whale, spends summer in polar waters scooping up krill. In winter, this whale migrates to warmer waters to breed. This 20-ton (18 t) whale sometimes leaps out of the water in a movement called breaching.

Penguins

There are 17 species of penguins. All live in the Southern Hemisphere, mostly in Antarctica and sub-Antarctica. The larger penguins, such as the emperor and king, live in the coldest regions. The smaller ones, such as the little blue penguin, live in more temperate zones. A few smaller penguins, including the Adélie, breed in Antarctica in summer in ice-free areas. Only the emperor breeds there over winter, the male holding the egg on his feet under a flap of feathered skin while his mate returns to sea to feed.

All penguins are excellent swimmers and dive for krill, fish, and squid. Their wings have flattened, heavy bones, which make them ideal as paddles. On land, however, penguins waddle or jump along awkwardly on short legs with webbed feet.

ICE ADAPTATIONS

Penguins have layers of blubber and downy under layers of feathers to trap body heat. Oily outer feathers with interlocking scales keep water out. Feathers cover as much of the birds' skin as possible, and long toenails help them grip the slippery ice.

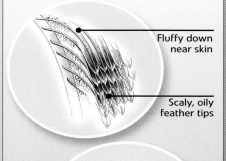

Fluffy down near skin

Scaly, oily feather tips

Ankle feathers

Long nails to grip ice

Huddling for warmth
Male emperor penguins spend winter on the Antarctic mainland. They survive by huddling together for warmth, each bird taking his turn on the outside.

Swimming emperors

While awkward on land, emperor penguins are fast and agile in the water. They can swim up to 20 miles per hour (32 km/h) and can stay underwater for as long as 22 minutes.

Watertight feathers
The chilly water cannot reach the penguin's skin, with its oily and watertight feathers..

Bubble trails
Penguins leave a trail of air bubbles behind them as they swim.

Fast swimmers
Starting at the tip of its pointed beak, the penguin's whole body is streamlined for fast swimming.

Flipper wings
Penguins look like they are flying underwater, with their stiff wings acting like paddles.

Polar Seals

Antarctic fur seal
This eared seal has thick fur, and the males have a thick "mane" around the neck.

Seals thrive in the cold polar regions, although some also live in temperate zones. All seals are superbly adapted to life in the water. They are streamlined and their limbs have become strong flippers, better suited to swimming than walking on land. Their flexible spines allow them to be highly maneuverable swimmers, able to turn quickly to chase fish or penguins or to dodge predators. Most seals have fur and layers of blubber to keep them warm in the icy water.

All seals come onto land or ice floes to breed, many forming colonies. Males are always larger than females. The males fight each other and establish territories within the colony and breed with several females. The mothers feed their pups rich milk. After several weeks, the pups must fend for themselves.

Spotted coat
The coat is darker above, lighter beneath, and spotted like the wild cat it is named for.

The solitary leopard seal

These fierce hunters usually roam the Antarctic waters alone, coming ashore only to breed. They eat krill but also seize penguins, other seabirds, and seal pups. Males and females call, perhaps to find each other.

Did You Know?

Seals can shut their nostrils when they swim. This stops water from entering their lungs. Some seals can remain underwater for as long as an hour.

Front flipper
Large, powerful front flippers allow the leopard seal to maneuver quickly while chasing prey.

Ears or no ears

There are two types of seals. Those with no outer ear flaps are called non-eared, or "true," seals. Their back flippers point backward. Those with outer ear flaps are called eared seals. Their back flippers point forward.

Crabeater seal

This true seal lives in Antarctic waters. It eats krill, not crabs, sieving them through its molars.

Large head

When it catches its prey, the seal shakes its large, powerful head to tear the prey into pieces small enough to swallow.

Three-pointed molars

Pointed top and bottom molars lock together to sieve krill from the water.

Giant jaws

The long jaws open wide and close powerfully, with long canine teeth sinking into larger prey.

Seabirds

L arge numbers of seabirds that fly live in the polar regions, exploiting the rich marine resources. Some, such as the wandering albatross, fly over the open ocean, whereas others, such as the southern giant petrel, concentrate on coastlines.

Seabirds eat a diverse range of foods. Albatrosses eat fish and squid. Arctic terns eat mainly fish, sometimes snatching them from other birds. Puffins specialize in catching small, schooling fish. Antarctic skuas catch their own fish but also snatch other seabirds' catches. They frequent penguin colonies, snatching unattended chicks and eggs. During the warmer months, most of these seabirds breed in colonies in protected places on islands and along cliff tops. Some, such as albatrosses, make mud nests, while others, such as puffins, nest in burrows.

Wide-winged
This albatross has the largest wingspan of any bird alive today. It reaches 11.5 feet (3.5 m).

Shoulder lock
The wings are held in an outstretched position with a locking mechanism in the shoulder, saving energy.

ARCTIC TERN

The arctic tern has the longest migration journey of any animal. After the summer breeding season in the Arctic, they undertake a three-month journey of some 25,000 miles (40,200 km) to Antarctica. They return north at the end of the southern summer.

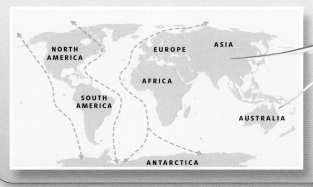

NORTH AMERICA

EUROPE

ASIA

AFRICA

SOUTH AMERICA

AUSTRALIA

ANTARCTICA

KEY
The arctic tern's migration route

Narrow wings
Long, narrow wings are perfect for effortless gliding and riding air currents above the ocean.

Wild wanderer

The wandering albatross can live for up to 80 years and spends much of its life gliding above the ocean, taking squid and fish from its surface. These birds breed on sub-Antarctic islands.

Tucked away
The feet lie flat behind the bird as it flies. This prevents drag that would slow it down.

Muscle power
Strong muscles attached to the breastbone provide power for flapping that is needed during takeoff.

Atlantic puffin
These sociable birds do most things together. They breed in colonies, dig burrows, rest standing together, and form "rafts" on the water and dive after schools of fish.

Did You Know?

The wandering albatross is a threatened species. They dive for lures on longline tuna fishing lines and are accidentally caught. Thousands die in this way each year.

Exploring the Polar Regions

People have long lived within the Arctic Circle, and early Viking explorers settled northern lands, such as Greenland, centuries ago. In the nineteenth century, explorers began to aim for the northernmost point of the world itself, the North Pole. A similar quest to reach the South Pole began just after the turn of the twentieth century. The extreme conditions led to many failures, and there was much to be learned about what clothing and other equipment was the most suitable. The North Pole was finally reached in 1909 and the South Pole in 1911.

Scientists continue to explore and learn about life in these amazing regions of Earth. They have even set up permanent bases in Antarctica. Tourists have also been drawn to venture into the polar regions, wanting to experience their extreme beauty firsthand.

Northern dash

In March 1909, an American team set off for the North Pole, preparing supply stations on the way. Six men made the final dash. They reached the pole on April 6.

The *Endurance*, 1915

Tourists
Tourists line the bow of an ice-breaking vessel to watch the ice crack as they head into the pack ice surrounding Antarctica.

Famous polar explorers

Many explorers traveled to the Arctic and Antarctica, some perishing in their attempts. Sometimes poor equipment and decisions were to blame, along with bad luck.

1827 William Edward Parry
A British expedition attempts to reach the North Pole but does not succeed.

1909 Robert Peary
An American team, including four experienced Inuit sleigh drivers, reaches the North Pole.

1911 Roald Amundsen
A Norwegian team using dog-drawn sleighs reaches the South Pole.

1912 Robert Falcon Scott
A British team reaches the South Pole on foot, perishing on the return journey.

1915 Sir Ernest Shackleton
The *Endurance* is trapped in pack ice and sinks, ending this Antarctic expedition.

1926 Roald Amundsen
The airship *Norge* makes the first flight over the North Pole.

1929 Richard Byrd
An airplane makes the first flight over the South Pole.

Glossary

adapted (uh-DAPT-ed)
Changed or altered to suit conditions or environments.

adjoining (uh-JOYN-ing)
Connecting or joining on to; right beside.

atmosphere
(AT-muh-sfeer) The layer of gases surrounding a planet, such as Earth.

buoyancy (BOY-unt-see)
The ability of an object to float in water.

camouflaged
(KA-muh-flahjd) Disguised in appearance in order to remain hidden. Color, shape, and patterns can help an animal be camouflaged in its environment.

carnivores
(KAHR-neh-vorz)
Animals that eat the flesh of other animals.

compacting
(kom-PAK-ting) Packing firmly together.

conical (KO-nih-kul)
Shaped like a cone.

continent (KON-tuh-nent)
One of seven large landmasses on Earth.

digestive (dy-JES-tiv)
Describes the breaking down of food into substances that can be absorbed by a plant or animal.

diminishes
(duh-MIH-nish-ez) Makes or becomes smaller or less.

dominated
(DAH-muh-nayt-ed)
Describes something that is the greatest part of something.

echolocation
(eh-koh-loh-KAY-shun)
A sensory system used by some animals where echoes of sounds made by the animal are picked up to find their way around or to locate prey.

fend (FEND) To survive and provide for oneself.

frequent (free-KWENT) To visit often.

hibernate (HY-bur-nayt)
To pass through the winter in a sleeplike state, where the body has a slowed heart rate and lower temperature. This ensures that an animal does not need as much energy to stay warm or active and can live off stored body fat.

insulates (IN-suh-layts)
Covers or wraps in a material or substance that stops heat from escaping or entering.

interlocking
(in-ter-LOK-ing) Linking or joining in some way as to be locked together.

invertebrates
(in-VER-teh-brets) Animals that do not have backbones.

maneuverable
(muh-NOO-veh-ruh-bel)
Readily able to change course.

nitrogen (NY-truh-jen)
A gas with no color or taste that makes up 78 percent of Earth's atmosphere and is found in all living organisms.

perishing (PER-ish-ing)
Dying or ceasing to exist.

permafrost
(PUR-muh-frost)
A layer of soil that is
permanently frozen.

permanently
(PER-muh-nint-lee) In a
way that lasts forever.

proteins (PROH-teenz)
Complex natural chains of
chemicals found in all living
things. All living things must
absorb proteins to allow their
own growth and repair.

reproduce
(ree-pruh-DOOS) To breed or
produce young.

resources (REE-sawrs-ez)
Things that are able to be
used for a purpose.

ruptures
(RUP-cherz) Bursts or tears
open or apart.

scavenging (SKA-venj-ing)
Feeding from an animal that
was already dead and did not
need to be killed by the one
eating its flesh.

strategies (STRA-tuh-jeez)
Plans or approaches to
carrying out an action, such
as hunting.

streamlined
(STREEM-lynd) Shaped so as
to have little resistance to
water or air and to be able to
move through either easily.

surplus (SUR-plus) An
amount greater than what is
necessary. Surplus food is
what is left over after basic
needs are met.

temperate (TEM-puh-rut)
Being moderate all the time
and not becoming either
extremely hot or cold.

venture (VEN-chur) To go
somewhere risking danger.

vulnerable
(VUL-neh-ruh-bel) Weak and
open to attack; at risk.

Index

A
albatrosses 26, 27
   wandering albatrosses 26, 27
Amundsen, Roald 29
Antarctica 8–9, 22, 26, 28, 29
Antarctic skuas 26
Arctic 6–7, 8, 10, 12, 17, 18,
   26, 29
Arctic Circle 6, 7, 8. 28
arctic foxes 14, 15
arctic hares 12, 15
Arctic Ocean 6, 20
arctic terns 26

B
beluga whales 16
blubber 16, 18, 20, 22, 24
Byrd, Richard 29

C
caribou 12, 13

E
Endurance 29

G
giant petrels 26
glacier 6, 8, 9

I
iceberg 6, 8

L
lemmings 12, 14, 15

N
North Pole 6, 28, 29

O
orcas 18, 20, 21

P
Parry, William Edward 29
penguins 22–23, 24
   Adélie penguins 22
   emperor penguins 22, 23
   king penguins 22
permafrost 14
polar bears 7, 13, 14, 16–17, 18

R
reindeer 12, 13, 16

S
Scott, Robert Falcon 29
sea ice 6, 7, 8, 16, 18
sea lions 20
seals 7, 16, 17, 20, 21, 24–25
   Antarctic fur seals 24
   crabeater seals 25
   leopard seals 24
Shackleton, Sir Ernest 29
snowy owls 14
South Pole 9, 28, 29
sundews 11

T
tourists 28, 29
tundra 10, 12, 13

W
walruses 18–19, 20
willow ptarmigans 15
wolves 13, 14

Websites

Due to the changing nature of Internet links, PowerKids Press has developed an online list of websites related to the subject of this book. This site is updated regularly. Please use this link to access the list: www.powerkidslinks.com/disc/arctic/